CW00571048

FISHING

Top Tackle Tips

POCKET GUIDES

COMPILED BY
**LAWRIE McENALLY
& JULIE McENALLY**

CONSULTANT EDITOR
STUART McLAUGHLIN

BayBooks

An imprint of HarperCollins*Publishers*

A Bay Books Publication

Bay Books, an imprint of
HarperCollins*Publishers*
25 Ryde Road, Pymble, Sydney, NSW 2073, Australia
31 View Road, Glenfield, Auckland 10, New Zealand

First published in Australia in 1993

National Library of Australia
Cataloguing-in-Publication data:

McEnally, Lawrie.
   Top tackle tips.

   Includes index.
   ISBN 1 86378 141 2.

   1. Fishing tackle. I. McEnally, Julie. II. Title.
   (Series: Fishing Australia pocket guides)

688.7912

The publishers gratefully acknowledge the assistance of the
many contributors to Fishing Australia

Cover photograph by Quentin Bacon
Cover styling by Louise Owens
Printed in Australia by The Griffin Press, Adelaide

9 8 7 6 5 4 3 2 1
96 95 94 93

CONTENTS

INTRODUCTION

A good understanding of fishing tackle is a vital part of the angler's craft. There are very few sports where so much tackle is either required or available. Indeed, the array of gear available in tackle shops today is quite staggering and, for many, bewildering.

The level of equipment required is however decided by the individual angler. Some go fishing with a couple of handlines, a packet of sinkers and hooks, a knife and some bait. Others need a utility just to cart their gear around.

Whatever your level of equipment, you need good advice. This handbook sets out the best ways to select, maintain and enjoy your tackle. It covers such matters as reel maintenance, selecting line, speciality hooks, and choosing hand tools.

But assembling the right tackle is only a first step in successful fishing; learning how to use the gear is the real key to more rewarding fishing and bigger catches. Thus we have included in this book information on a variety of techniques that can be used in specific fishing situations, from freshwater trolling to bluewater spincasting.

Top Tackle Tips has been prepared by experienced fishing writers who operate at the cutting edge of fishing tackle technology and who work work hard at their chosen sport. Their experience and understanding of the needs of anglers make the information in this book invaluable.

All anglers, from first timers to old hands, will value *Top Tackle Tips* as the esssential quick-reference guide they can turn to again and again for answers to their most frequent queries about effective fishing tackle.

The right tackle combined with the right techniques will lead to impressive catches like this.

REEL MAINTENANCE

Modern reels of medium to high quality are usually in excellent condition straight from the box. The days of having to tune a reel after purchasing it are gone. Keeping the reel in good operating condition through its working life then becomes the job of the angler.

The most harmful element in fishing is salt, which will cause corrosion in most metals. Sand, dirt and dust are also problems that must be countered.

Unfortunately most reels are not sealed, so both salt and sand can enter the workings of the reel. To stop damage by salt and sand there are a number of simple steps that should be followed at the end of each fishing session.

The only other type of reel problem occasionally faced by anglers is wear or breakage. These problems can be the result of poor maintenance, part failure, accident or just normal wear and tear. Good service will avoid most of these problems by detecting worn parts early.

BASIC MAINTENANCE

All reels, no matter how expensive need care and attention. Even seemingly simple, robust reels like the sidecast need some basic maintenance at the end of a day's fishing.

The best method is to wash the reel under a gently running hose or tap. Lever drag game reels are an exception and should not be washed in this way, as water could penetrate the drag system. These are best wiped over with a damp rag.

Do not have the water gushing over the reel as this can cause damage by forcing salt and dirt into the reel. A light stream of water is fine for washing the salt off.

After washing, shake the reel and allow a little time for it to drip-dry. Once the reel is dry, wipe it over with a slightly oily rag. Don't overdo the use of oil or grease, as this material can actually hold salt and dirt if applied too thickly — lightly does it!

As mentioned above, game reels should be wiped down with a damp cloth or towel, followed up with a wipe with an oily cloth or a light spray of aerosol lubricant.

The only part of most reels that needs regular oiling is the handle. The rest of the reel can be done when doing full strip downs, although the occasional drop of oil on the Archimedean screw of your baitcaster's level wind is also a good idea.

FULL STRIP DOWN

Reels need to be stripped down in order to be cleaned and greased. How often this should be done depends on how often the reel is used. If the reel is only used once a month, then it probably only needs a full service once every year or two. If the reel is used every weekend, then it should get a service every three or four months.

The aim of the service is prevent future breakdowns and to keep the reel operating smoothly. There is nothing more frustrating than having a reel that is not operating properly. Worse still it can cost fish and fishing time.

No matter what type of reel is to be serviced, it is important to follow the manufacturer's manual. Mechanical aptitude varies from person to person but, if a logical progression is followed, all reels can easily be stripped down and reassembled.

Always work on a clean, flat surface and lay out the pieces in order as you take the reel apart.

As each part is removed from the reel, wash it thoroughly in white spirit and then place it on some newspaper to dry. The tiny ball bearings in fishing reels need particular care and should be cleaned with a little brush to remove any dirt.

The main workings of the reel should be easy to clean; just take note of where each piece came from as you work along. If the reel will not strip down past a certain point without force then you have a problem that is best fixed by a tackle shop. The general rule is not to force anything unless you are certain it is supposed to move.

Clean the drag washers and apply a very light smear of grease to the metal washers — a special silicon lube is available for this purpose.

A basic tool kit is all that's needed for a strip down and service.

Work on a clean, flat surface and lay all parts out neatly, in the order they are disassembled.

Removing the end plate of a baitcaster to reveal the spool and anti-backlash brake blocks

The workings of a baitcaster. Note the drag washers inside the main gear.

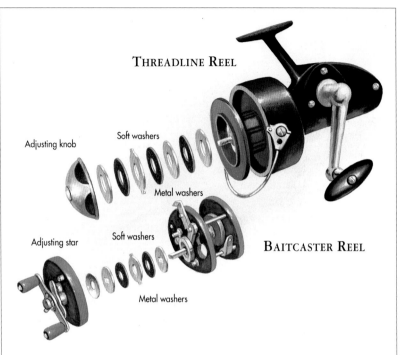

THREADLINE REEL

Adjusting knob

Soft washers

Metal washers

BAITCASTER REEL

Adjusting star

Soft washers

Metal washers

Typical drag assemblies

The rest of the reel goes back together the same way it came apart. Most parts only need a little smear of grease for protection, but the bearings should be packed with light grease using finger pressure. The main shaft in a threadline and the meshing face of the gears can also use a little extra grease.

As a rule, oil should only be used as a point lubricant, as overuse of oil can have it running into places where it is not needed, like the drag. Stay with grease for internal lubrication. A little oil on the bail arm springs of threadlines and in the reel handle can be useful but, on the whole, oil should

be used for exterior protection only.

Once the reel is back together, check all the functions to make sure everything is working properly for the next outing.

With a little practice, stripping down any reel is a simple job. The hassles usually happen on the first try. With patience and common sense, any reel can easily be cleaned and relubricated in a very short time.

Like any piece of machinery, fishing reels need service to perform at their best, and the angler must have reels that are operating properly in order to enjoy the fishing and catch fish.

FISHING REEL DRAG SYSTEMS

Although there are many types of reels on the market, the drag systems in most are remarkably similar. Reels like threadlines, baitcasters and larger, revolving drum reels all use a multi-washer drag. Even lever drag game reels use a washer system, though they have fewer washers and need finer tuning than most other systems.

The basic requirement of a drag system is that it should pay out line smoothly under load as the tension from the fish reaches the desired strength setting on the reel. To operate properly, the drag surface must be as flat and clean as possible.

Nothing is more annoying than tackle that loses fish, and it is through bad drags that many fish, especially very large ones, are lost.

COMMON DRAG FAULTS

Some drags need a lot more tension than is set by the angler to start rolling. This is known as a sticky drag, and is usually caused by corrosion or dirt build up.

Some drags are bumpy and rough, alternatively slipping and grabbing as the fish runs. This is caused by water in the system or too much oil or grease.

Other problems are caused by uneven or high spots on the metal washers. This produces a chattering drag that pays out line in rapid, uneven jerks.

An internal view of a typical threadline reel

PREVENTATIVE MEDICINE

The best way to keep a drag operating smoothly is to carry out preventative maintenance before any problems set in. As most quality reels will have good drags when new, they can be kept that way for a long time with a just a little care and some regular maintenance.

The first thing is to make sure that the reel is not exposed to great torrents of sea water. This sort of drenching usually occurs while trolling in choppy seas, particularly in small boats, or when rods are left in rod holders while running in heavy weather conditions. Don't dunk reels in sea water at any time, and always remove them from rod holders when travelling home. Always back the drag off when you put a reel away as a set drag will quickly buckle or warp the drag washers.

SERVICING YOUR DRAG

The first point to be made is that different quality reels will have different quality drags. A cheap supermarket reel may have a drag system that will never work properly, simply because of the standard of material used in its construction. A quality reel will have a good drag that can be tuned if necessary.

To service the drag, you need the specialised reel tools supplied by the manufacturer, plus white spirit or some other solvent, wet and dry sandpaper and some very light reel grease.

For full instructions, *see* **Reel Maintenance**, pp. 5–7.

DRAG SETTINGS

With the drag system working smoothly, the important part of the process is to set

Bench testing a gamefishing reel's drag

the drag correctly. It must be firm enough to hook and fight the fish effectively without applying so much strain that the line will break. There is really no excuse for the angler breaking the line.

SETTING THE DRAG THROUGH THE ROD

Rather than measuring drag straight off the spool, it's a far better idea to measure it off the rod tip.

By setting the rod in a holder and using a spring balance, the actual working drag when fighting a fish can be measured. Game anglers do this as a matter of habit. Most strike and fighting drags are set at one quarter of the line's rated breaking strain (for example, 6 kg strain on 24 kg line).

After line leaves the reel, actual drag against the fish is increased by friction caused by line passing over the runners. Naturally, the amount of extra drag depends upon the number and efficiency of the runners.

How hard you pull against the rod will also affect the actual drag, by increasing or decreasing friction on the runners. When a fish is running fast, the rod should not be pulled back hard, as this will often break the line. It is better to keep enough bend in the rod to gain some cushioning against sudden surges or acrobatics without forcing anything.

Drag settings need careful assessment. The pressure needs to be firm but not harsh. Line should pay out well before drag pressure forces the line to break.

CHANGING THE DRAG WHILE FIGHTING A FISH

Lever drags and other pre-set systems are designed to allow drag alterations within a pre-determined range of settings while actually fighting a fish.

This can be done with conventional star drag systems, albeit without the same degree of surety as to just how much drag is being eased or increased. A spot of something like red nail polish on one arm of the star wheel is a great help in this, as you can then deduce drag alterations from the movement of the 'red dot'.

Game fishermen talk of strike drag — a lesser drag setting aimed at minimising chances of a break-off in those first moments when a hooked fish is thrashing about and possibly jumping wildly. Later, when the fish tires and the chances of high speed antics are reduced, the drag setting is increased. These later stages of the fight are where many fish go deep and slug it out against line pressure.

When it all comes down to it, even the best of drags is only able to operate as well as the person using it.

THE EFFECTS OF LINE LOSS

The loss of a significant amount of line off the spool can dramatically increase a carefully set drag.

As line pours off the spool, the diameter of the line load decreases, effectively reducing the amount of leverage the line (where it's coming off the spool) has against the drag. Unless the drag setting is decreased accordingly as line unloads, a break-off becomes increasingly likely.

Another factor to be considered is the actual drag of the line itself in the water behind the fish. Fish rarely take off in a straight line — more often there is a huge belly of line trailing in the water behind the running fish. This type of problem is experienced with long-running fish on light tackle. Drag settings must be lowered as the line level shrinks.

KEEPING THE DRAG SYSTEM DRY

Drags of all kinds are sensitive to water. They often grab or become jerky after they have received a soaking and water has entered the system. Even the highest grade materials like teflon and split-chrome leather can be adversely affected by either fresh or salt water.

To prevent water entering the drag mechanism when washing or hosing down your reels after a day's fishing, ensure that the drag knob or star wheel is screwed up tight. Remember, however, to back it right off once the reel has dried out, otherwise the washers will compress and spoil the drag's performance next time you're out fishing.

A tip for anglers who regularly go to sea with the rods in rod holders that inevitably receive a 'drowning': try placing an elasticised shower cap over the reels to help keep water out of the drag. These little raincoats are not expensive and can be a great drag saver.

Polythene, in the form of a plastic bag or shower cap, can be used to keep your reel dry and protect it from the effects of salt water.

MONOS
AIN'T MONOS

Right now, anglers have access to a great range of widely different, nylon fishing lines. While they are all monofilament nylon lines, their behaviour and characteristics vary widely from brand to brand.

The categories available include general purpose, thin for breaking strain, thick for breaking strain, hard exterior, soft exterior, limp, stiff, high stretch and limited stretch. All are available in a range of colours.

With so much choice, it is often difficult for the average angler to decide which line suits his or her particular purpose. What the angler needs to know is what lines suit what style of fishing best, and what factors to do with line affect each fishing situation.

BREAKING STRAIN AND DIAMETER

There are two basic measures of a fishing line. One is its physical breaking strain and the other is its diameter. As a general rule the two are interrelated.

An average 6 kg breaking strain line has a diameter of about 0.35 mm. Very specialised lines which offer great strength for diameter, may have a diameter of 0.26 mm on a 6 kg line. Usually the thin, very strong lines have low abrasion resistance because of their small surface area.

One advantage of very fine line is that it allows longer casts on threadlines and sidecast reels, as the line drag over the spool lip is reduced and the line load stays higher on the reel during the cast. Other advantages include the fact that more line can be put on the spool and — in very fine line classes — smaller lures can be cast more easily.

Some anglers reverse the process so they can have greater line strength while staying with their usual line diameter.

Sport and game fishermen need accurately tested lines to qualify their fish for various line classes. To meet this demand, many manufacturers are selling pre-tested or stated-strength lines that meet the needs of line class anglers.

Game fishermen also tend to use line that is fairly thick for breaking strain in order to cope with the wear and tear of long fights.

LINE STRETCH

Another important point is the amount of stretch in a line. All nylon lines have some stretch. Some very soft lines can actually have so much stretch that it is hard to sink the hook.

Anglers working lures on fish that head for the snags need to use low stretch lines for more direct hook-up and greater fish control. A stretchy line may allow the fish to reach the snag without the angler losing any line off the reel.

Low stretch lines can have their faults too. If the angler makes a mistake when fighting a fish on average line, the stretch may allow enough time to back off before the line breaks. With limited stretch lines, no such margin is available. Push the line too far and it breaks. So each type of line has its pros and cons.

SURFACE STRENGTH

The physical hardness of the line — particularly its exterior or surface — will affect its abrasion resistance. This is not the same as line stiffness, which is an entirely different issue. Put simply, some lines have a harder exterior than others due to their chemical composition.

Hard exteriors make for good fishing in tough country. Rock anglers learn very quickly about the abrasion resistance of

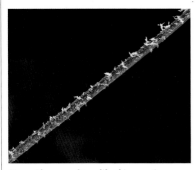

To avoid wear and tear like this occurring quickly, lines with a hard exterior are recommended.

nylon. Game and sport anglers also need tough nylon exteriors on their trace material. In fact, several manufacturers have produced trace materials with superb abrasion resistance.

'MEMORY' AND STIFFNESS

The stiffness of a line is indicated by how it sits on a reel, or on the deck of a boat if using a handline. Some line has the unruly behaviour of fencing wire when placed on a spool. It wants to jump off the reel in great coils and always lies in those coils when in use.

The coils are referred to as 'memory', as the line retains the shape of the spool it was on and will not lie straight when pressure is eased. In cold conditions this sort of line becomes unmanageable.

Excess stiffness is usually found in very cheap lines; major brands do not suffer from the problem.

KNOT STRENGTH

Many anglers worry about the knot strength of their line, rather than the quality of the knots they tie. It is important to state that all recognised brands of line seem to have good knot strength.

Given that most of the lines are suitable, it is almost always the angler's fault when the line gives way due to knot failure.

As a guide though, the lines most prone to failure under stress are the super soft, very supple types. These lines often slip a little under extreme stress and if the tag end of the knot has not been left just a little exposed, it may pull through. Generally though, well-tied knots do not move much.

LINE COLOUR

The use of coloured lines is a source of fierce debate among anglers. No fishing line is invisible, but some are less visible than others.

The only colours that the authors have seen positively rejected by fish under some conditions are the fluorescent yellows and oranges used for game and sport fishing.

These lines are used so that the skipper can see them during the fight. As a trace is almost always used in game fishing, the line colour does not matter, but it may affect bait fishing situations.

SPECIAL FEATURES

Developments over the next few years are likely to include new lines with special features for a particular type of fishing.

The market for general-purpose lines is totally saturated.

Factors that are advantageous to specific forms of angling will be incorporated into various lines. For example, specifically-designed lines for bluewater fishing will become more common. Developments like this will of course help anglers perform better in their chosen field.

Lure casters are being targeted now with a couple of new high-strength, small diameter lines that also have limited stretch, high abrasion resistance and very long wear when casting. This trend will grow as the various markets are explored.

For the average angler there are so many good lines available, that it is hard to pick a poor performer. Stay with name brands and the results should be good.

For anglers with specific performance demands for their lines, the age of designer lines is here and further innovations are on the way. Maybe even a line that the fish can't see!

Brightly-coloured lines have advantages and disadvantages. In game fishing they allow the skipper to see the line during a fight.

SPECIALITY HOOKS

Some of the most important advances in modern fishing technology have been in fish hooks. Both in Japan and Europe there has been a trend to smaller, lighter, specialist-designed fish hooks.

Advances in both metallurgy and production processes have meant very rapid changes. The results of these changes are now very visible on tackle shop shelves.

The question for anglers is, what benefits do they get from these hooks? Here are some of the facts.

CHEMICAL SHARPENING

The use of chemical sharpening has meant such hooks now come out of the packet with a genuinely sharp point. Standard hooks are actually quite blunt and need a touch with a sharpening stone or file to perform properly. Chemically sharpened hooks need no sharpening.

The difference in sharpness between a quality chemically sharpened hook and a quality standard hook is significant, and definitely offers a real advantage when hooking the fish.

HOOK GAUGE

Advances in metallurgy have also led to some of the new lightweight hook designs being unbelievably strong for their size. This strength is achieved by combining intrinsically strong patterns with vastly improved raw stock.

The advantage for the angler is that smaller hooks can be used to fool smart fish. Alternatively, lighter gauge hooks can also be used to improve bait presentation.

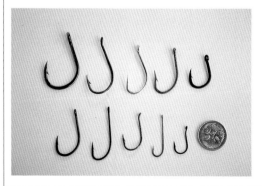

Speciality hooks come in a range of sizes that covers everything from yellowfin tuna to luderick.

Fishing for bream and luderick has been enormously improved by lighter gauge hooks being available. Specialist presentations, such as mudeyes on tiny hooks for trout, have also been greatly advanced. Game fishing and sport fishing have benefited from several new ranges of hooks for live baiting and for working pilchards and strip baits for yellowfin tuna.

COLOURED HOOKS

There are some times when coloured hooks can make a difference. It is not clear whether fish actually see colour or just the reflection of the coloured metal, but it seems, particularly in heavily fished areas with clear water, that the fish may be fooled if the colour of the hook blends in with the colour of the bait. A wide variety of colours is available and it is just a matter of selecting the right one for your bait.

See also **Colour and the Angler**, pp. 20–21.

PATTERNS

Many new hook patterns have also been introduced to the market in recent years. These patterns have mostly been developed to suit fish species in other countries but they have applications in Australia and New Zealand as well.

Most anglers are comfortable with the traditional patterns like Suicide, Limerick, Longshank and so on, but there are already several new patterns that will stay in use and become more popular with the passing of time.

Hooks like the Daiichi Eastern Estuary hook, the Gamakatsu Live Bait HD and the Mustad Laser Tech are available at many tackle shops and have plenty to offer keen anglers.

Tru-turn hooks are a novel twist on the traditional hook theme. The shank of the hook is keyed sideways so that the point of the hook turns into the jaw of the fish when the hook is set. These hooks come in some useful patterns and may help hook extra fish.

The real answer to the hook problem though is to ensure that the hook suits its intended purpose. New technology, no matter how smart, cannot replace the essential ingredients of good fishing. The fish still have to take the bait before the hook can do the job.

Tru-turn hooks have a distinctively shaped shank designed to set the hook more effectively.

SALTWATER TROLLING LURES

Right around the coastline many anglers use a variety of lures in the hope of catching a passing fish's eye. In many locations, the fishing is for first-rate table fish, in others it's purely an exercise in bait gathering while, at the other end of the scale, some anglers are trying to attract large game fish.

However, in all cases the reasoning behind the use of lures remains basically the same: each lure is trolled in the hope of imitating a fish which will be fancied by another hungry fish. The first essential is that the lure must be similar to what the fish in the area like to eat. Other variables include the lure type, and the depth and speed at which the lure is worked.

By putting together a package of lures and the appropriate tackle, anglers can bag a good supply of fish on most outings. There are several 'families' of trolling lures and each has a specific application. The major groups are minnows, spoons and skirted or feather lures.

MINNOWS

Minnow lures are superb fish catchers in almost all situations. Their fish-like shape and 'wounded' action make them attractive to most fish.

The vibrating, fish-like action is a result of the bib at the head of the lure. Pressure on the bib as it's drawn through the water dictates the action. The size of the bib also

Minnow lures will provide a range of captures including fish like this kingfish.

dictates how deep the lure will run. Working a lure 3 or 4 metres below the surface can be a tremendous advantage for trapping deepwater predators.

As well as being effective at slower speeds, high quality minnow lures can be trolled at speeds of up to 10 knots. The combination of action and speed makes them a good choice for the capture of almost all species of predatory fish. An exception is billfish, which rarely stay hooked because the treble hook setup on minnow lures gives these twisting, turning fighters enough leverage to throw the hook. However, minnow lures swim through the water without twisting, which can be a problem with other trolling lures.

To rig a minnow lure the only thing needed is a metre or so of nylon trace, usually about three times as strong as the breaking stain of the main line. In areas where the fish have plenty of teeth, a light wire trace must be considered. The lure is connected to the trace by a snap swivel and the trace to the main line by either a swivel or a solid brass ring.

Minnow lures may need fine tuning to get them to swim upright, particularly at high speeds. This tuning is done by adjusting the metal eyelet at the front of the lure, gently bending it towards the same side the lure is leaning to in the water. Most minnow manufacturers have tuning instructions either on, or in, the lure packaging.

Bibless minnows get their action by having the towing eyelet set at the balance point of the lure. Bibless minnows can be trolled at high speeds of up to 15 knots.

METAL SPOONS AND JIGS

These lures get their action from water running over their curved or raised surfaces. Most of these lures are limited by design to speeds of less than three or four knots. With a few exceptions, spoons are not used a great deal in modern, bluewater trolling situations, except in areas where Spanish mackerel are common.

A close associate of the spoon or metal jig is the plastic trolling lure known as the Smith's or Halco Tuna jig. This simple, boat-shaped lure is very effective on a wide range of surface-feeding fish.

HEADED AND SKIRTED LURES

This category of lures includes plastic squids, feathers and combinations of hard heads with a variety of body materials. All these lures are designed to give a bait-like imitation when dragged through the water. Also in this group are the sophisticated gamefishing lures. Large flies designed for saltwater fishing can also be included in this category.

Many of the lures in this family have no particular action at all but simply run straight through the water just below the surface. They are attractive to predatory fish because they look like a bait fish and are usually fished at medium to fast speeds to give the fish a hit or miss proposition.

Konaheads, knuckleheads and all sorts of other heads are available that do have an action which is provided by water passing over the face of the lure. The action is governed by the speed at which the lure is pulled through the water. The faster the speed the more action, but only up to a certain point beyond which the lure starts to get airborne.

These skirted lures are usually trolled at 3 to 10 knots, although some patterns will stay in the water up to 18 knots. Most of the larger game fish are quite capable of catching lures at this speed.

The lures are rigged by passing the trace through the head and securing the hook or hooks as required. The hook is usually placed so that the point is right in the end fronds of the skirt. Often beads or a small crimp are used as a spacer to correctly position the hook. Hooks without a set, that is with the barb in line with the shank, must be used with trolling lures to avoid line twist.

The trace material can be either wire or nylon depending on the area being fished. As a general rule, wire is only used in tropical areas or for specific species such as wahoo, mackerel and barracouda. Lures generally catch more fish when rigged on nylon traces.

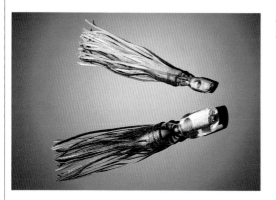

Skirted lures can be trolled at high speeds to tempt game fish.

COLOUR AND THE ANGLER

Anglers and scientists have always argued over whether fish actually see colour or simply interpret various colours in relation to the available light. Most experienced anglers will argue that there are colours that catch fish and there are combinations of lure colours and light and water clarity conditions that need definite consideration.

If you have one red lure and one blue lure out and the red lure is taking five strikes to every one on the blue then, so long as the lures are identical, the fish are showing a definite preference for the red under the prevailing conditions.

Remember however that conditions vary markedly from day to day, so try to remember a few of the general 'rules' relating to colour, as they can take some of the guesswork out of colour selection.

THE RULES OF COLOUR

Chrome and silver lures are standard colours for lures and work well in most conditions. However, there are a number of situations when other colours must be considered.

DULL DAY–DULL LURE

On overcast days, in slightly dingy water and early and late in the day, a fish is more likely to see a silhouette than light reflected off a chrome lure. You should therefore consider dull or dark lures. The closer your presentation will be fished to the surface the more important this is.

Good dull-day colours are dark blue, black, brown, rust red, grey and purple. By all means add some contrast (see below), but go for a dark effect overall.

Red and pink lures are regular fish takers.

Bright Day–Bright Lure

The opposite of the dull day–dull lure rule. Bright colours do work on a bright day, especially in clear water and with near-surface presentations.

Top bright-day colours are silver, chrome, red, yellow, green, chartreuse, white or even clear. A touch of dark such as stripes, spots or a tail can offer contrast which may sometimes do the trick.

Black at Night

At night you will have to depend on the fish seeing silhouettes. Therefore the best night-time lures and flies are all black or very dark, reasonably bulky and strong-actioned. If sunset is not yet complete, choose dark brown, dark grey, purple or dark blue.

Black on the Surface

With surface lures generally, it's a good idea to exploit the silhouette effect. Opt for solid, primary colours and avoid bright or transparent bellies, except on the ficklest of fish in the clearest and shallowest of waters.

The Colour Purple

Purple is a hot colour at dawn, particularly in salt water. It's not bad again at dusk, but it really shines from an hour before sun up until an hour after.

Fluoro in Dirty Water

Brightly fluorescent colours work best in dirty, muddy and discoloured water. The filthier the water, the brighter the lure needs to be. After all, a fish needs to be able to find your lure to eat it.

The best dingy-water fluorescent tones are bright yellow, chartreuse, lime green, orange and red.

Naturals in Clear Water

Most fish — especially less aggressive ones — respond much better to the so-called 'naturalised' colours and patterns in clear and very clear water.

In clear fresh water, think blacks, browns, fawns, pale orange and dark green. In the salt, look to blues, greens, silvers, white and clear finishes.

Silver and Gold

Many experienced trout fishermen swear by silver spinners in clear water and gold or brass ones in discoloured lakes or streams (remember silver and chrome can only reflect light). Copper, brass and gold give a deeper flash in coloured water.

Contrast

It is nearly always worth adding a touch of contrast — dark spots or bars on a light lure and light highlights on a dark one. This improves visibility, yet breaks up hard outlines.

Countershading and Oddballs

Throw a fish a curved ball every now and then, particularly when things are tough. Try reverse countershading — lures that are dark below and light above. It's unnatural, it stands out and it often gets eaten.

Hot pink and bright lime greens fall into the 'curved ball' category too.

But remember that colour is not the only factor in lure selection, just one side of a many-sided argument. Presentation, matching what the fish are eating, troll speed, lure action and how the lure is rigged are all just as important. If the other factors are right, then colour will play its part effectively.

WORKING WITH WIRE

Two types of wire are used in making wire traces. They are single strand wire and multi-strand wire.

Single strand is available in a variety of diameters from 5 kg up to stuff used on sharks, which could literally be used as fencing wire.

Both stainless steel and zinc- or cadmium-coated mild steel single strand wires are used for fishing. Special pre-straightened single strand wire sold in tackle stores comes in coils that if unravelled carefully won't coil up. Multi-strand wire is similarly sold in many different diameters.

The main differences between the two lie in rigging techniques, relative diameter to breaking strain, and flexibility.

SINGLE STRAND

Rigging is where single strand really shines. A properly executed single wire wrap is neater than any method of fastening the ends of multi-strand wire, plus it gives a 100 per cent knot strength, which allows the use of very fine wire traces. These are believed by many anglers to be less visible than a thick, mono nylon leader used for the same purpose.

To rig single strand, the only equipment needed is a pair of pliers with wire cutters

fitted. Parallel jaw pliers are the best.

When forming wraps it is absolutely vital that both wires wrap around each other, not one around the other. Once twisted round six to eight times, the wrap is finished off with four to six barrel rolls, this time with the tag end rolling neatly around the standing part. A small crank is then bent with the pliers. When bent back against the roll of the wire, the crank breaks off neatly without leaving a protrusion to jag fingers and clothing.

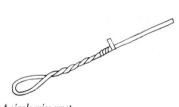

A single wire wrap

MULTI-STRAND

Multi-strand wire is more flexible than single strand, which makes it the better choice for active lures such as skirted, trolling lures.

Multi-strand wire is either plastic-coated or plain. Both of these types can be crimped. Some plastic-coated wires can also be tied by using flame to melt the plastic coating on the tag end and forming a twisted weld which will have 100 per cent knot strength if the weld is properly made. The twisted weld is almost as neat as a mono wire wrap and there's the added advantage of being able to actually tie nylon line to multi-strand wire.

The key to terminating multi-strand wire is the Flemish Eye — a special loop knot used whenever multi-strand is being terminated by either a twisted weld or a crimp. Without a Flemish Eye neither a

Flemish eye

crimp nor a twisted weld can be considered 100 per cent reliable.

Depending on the comparative diameter of wires to nylon, either a Huffnagle or Allbright knot will join line or leader directly to the wire trace. This eliminates hardware at the vulnerable join between nylon and wire — something of great benefit in parts of Australia where mackerel, wahoo, barracuda or other razor-

equipped fish are liable to take a shine to a swivel, or even the bubbles formed around a loop in the end of the wire.

Crimps are an easy way of terminating either plain or plastic-coated multi-strand wire. Their great advantages are speed and ease of use in inexperienced hands. Care must be taken however in selecting the correct size of crimp, otherwise they may slip.

If you're targeting fish with teeth, like this wolf herring, then you will have to use a wire trace.

GAFFS

Getting a good fish to the boat is just part of the game; bringing it safely aboard can be another story. Making sure you have the correct gaff for the situation is fundamental to successful angling. There can be no more frustrating experience in fishing than losing a prized catch because of an inadequate gaff.

It doesn't matter whether you are fishing from a boat, from a high rock platform, from a pier or a beach, there's a gaff available that is suited to your needs.

GAFFS FOR THE BOAT FISHERMAN

Boat gaffs fall into two major categories: those which are used for general offshore fishing, and those which are designed and built purposely for game species.

General-purpose boat gaffs come in a range of sizes. The most useful is a small gaff with a hook gape of around 6 cm. This is ideal for dealing with the likes of snapper, mulloway, kings and salmon.

A beefer version with a 10 cm-wide hook is suited to larger fish over 10 kg. Both sizes normally have a handle around 1 metre long, made of aluminium, cane, fibreglass or heavy dowel, to which the head or hook is solidly fixed.

Aluminium-handled boat gaffs are usually the most expensive type, but they are strong, light and resistant to corrosion.

GAMEFISH GAFFS

Gaffs for offshore game fishing need to be of the highest quality, as they will be subjected to all sorts of pressure from big, active fish over the course of many seasons.

Large fixed-head gaffs with gapes of up to 20 cm are used by game fishermen, but these are replaced by a detachable head or flying gaff when dealing with big sharks, marlin and other species which are likely to misbehave near the boat.

A turrum is landed using a light boat gaff.

The hook on the flying gaff is attached to a length of strong rope. When the hook is driven home, the head pulls free of the handle and the fish is controlled on the rope. This is far more practical and much safer than trying to subdue a thrashing shark or marlin with an aluminium handle flailing around your head!

ROCK FISHING GAFFS

Rock gaffs are of two popular varieties. The first and most basic is a long-handled type with a fixed hook, basically an elongated version of the general-purpose boat gaff. Handles for these are normally of stout rangoon cane, fibreglass or aluminium. Aluminium handles can also be purchased in threaded lengths which screw together to make the required length.

Although an awkward item to transport, the long pole rock gaff is very effective on snapper, mulloway and small to medium game fish.

Two styles of drop or cliff gaffs are also used extensively by rock fishermen around Australia. A basic drop gaff consists of three suitable hooks welded together with an ring at the top for attaching line. A rope of appropriate length and weight is tied to this ring. The whole device resembles a grapnel. These are used widely where the platform being fished is high above the water.

A refined version of the drop gaff has been in use for some time in Western Australia, where there is great demand for pinning big fish from very high locations.

The West Oz cliff gaff is basically of similar design to the three-pronged model already mentioned, but incorporates a line guide to facilitate more accurate placement from high ledges.

Both the drop gaff and the long-handled pole gaff also lend themselves perfectly to jetty or wharf situations.

BEACH GAFFS

Because the surf fisherman is able to fight the fish from sea level, gaffing from the beach doesn't normally present as many problems as gaffing in other fishing situations.

Apart from the relatively few anglers who chase sharks and rays in the surf, it is mainly the mulloway specialist who needs to consider a gaff for the beach. A short-handled, fixed-head gaff is all that is required. These normally feature a rubber, EVA or Hypalon hand grip and leather wrist strap.

GAFF MAINTENANCE

As with most tackle items, gaffs need some regular maintenance if they are to remain in good working order.

As soon as the coating on a galvanised gaff hook is broken, as when the point is sharpened on a stone or file, corrosion begins. It is wise to check the points of such hooks frequently, and to touch them up regularly to retain sharpness. A smear of grease or vaseline on the point will help resist rust.

FISHING KNIVES AND SCALERS

Fishing knives are an essential part of any angler's tackle. They are used to cut bait, trim knots, open split shot, remove hooks and to clean the catch. They are also handy in emergencies when something (line caught round someone's arm, for example) needs to be cut quickly.

In fact, knives are so important that fishermen actually need two to get most jobs done properly. One knife is a robust model for handling the work side of fishing like cutting bait and berley and other rough jobs. The second knife is strictly for neatly cleaning the catch.

WORKING KNIVES

They usually have a short, 15 cm blade, which is stiff, strong and able to handle heavy work. The grip should be solid and robust, yet feel comfortable to hold. Many models suitable for this type of work have a serrated edge on the back of the blade which is used for scaling.

As this style of knife will occasionally be misused or roughly treated, the quality need not be terribly high, although ultra-cheap knives are not worth having either. Knives in the mid-price bracket are the best bet.

A work knife should also come with some form of sheath or scabbard to enable the angler to put it on a belt when fishing. Having the blade close at hand saves time, can be an important safety measure, and avoids those irritating occasions when you have to search the whole boat for a cutting tool.

A fishing knife should be kept in a sheath when not in use.

Cleaning Knives

Of all the chores related to a good day's fishing, cleaning the catch is usually the last thing done. Nothing makes this job quicker or easier than a good knife.

A good cleaning knife should suit the type of fish being regularly handled. It should hold its edge and be easy to sharpen. Many anglers simply buy one utility knife and make it do a wide range of jobs. This works, but a good cleaning knife which is well suited to the task makes life much easier.

Anglers have such a wide choice of blades available, that selecting the right knife can be difficult. For most jobs such as gutting and filleting, a fairly stiff yet fine 15 to 22 cm blade is the best option.

Fillet knives with flexible blades are handy for working on small fish which have wide body shapes. Fish like bream, snapper, morwong and John dory can be filleted very well with this type of knife. The only problem with flexible blades is their lack of cutting power on bones. Heavy rib bones may present a problem but, on smaller fish, the ability of the knife to follow body contours can assist greatly.

With any fillet knife, the blade should be long enough to reach right across the width of the body. This makes the job easier by producing the fillet with one run of the knife.

Boning Knives

Boning knives are very good on large fish over about 5 kg. The power of the boning knife's blade enables it to get through tough skin, breast bones, heavy ribs and even the spine of some fish when cutlets are being produced. The turned-up point of a boning knife also allows it to handle tricky jobs around the gills and spine with minimal effort.

Knife Construction

All fishing knives should be of one-piece construction. Pen knives and utility knives are not generally suited to the hard work and equally harsh environment encountered when fishing.

Most blades are of stainless steel these days and although this type of steel does not hold an edge as well as some hard steels, the corrosion resistance compensates for a lot of extra sharpening.

Handles need to be comfortable and slip resistant. Both wood and formed plastic are excellent. A comfortable shape is probably the most important factor. As a general rule, filleting and boning knives should have fairly bulky handles to give plenty of grip.

With knives, price is usually some guide to quality, and spending a few extra dollars on a good knife will pay big dividends over time.

Keeping a Knife Sharp

No matter how sharp a knife is when purchased, it will not stay that way long once in use. In fact, a really sharp knife used for cleaning will need a touch on a stone or steel every 10 fish or so, and a bait knife should be sharpened at least once a day.

The choice of a sharpening stone or a steel is up to the individual, although for ease of use and because it does not corrode, a sharpening stone is probably better. Again, a quality, fine-grained stone is better than the coarse carborundum models used to sharpen hooks.

When using a stone, keep it wet and work the blade at an angle of about 15 degrees to the stone. Fine grain stones take longer to sharpen the blade than coarse grain stones because they remove less metal with each pass, but they do produce a smoother, longer-lasting edge.

SCALERS

A vast array of scalers is available to help make cleaning fish a little bit easier. Many general-purpose fishing knives have scalers built into the back of them, while other more specialised scalers are produced as separate items.

Most scalers are made of a serrated metal sheet with a comfortable handle. The idea is to provide a surface which lifts and removes fish scales quickly and easily.

Fish scalers are very cheap and as such are worth leaving in the tackle box, boat or boot of the car for those days when a big cleaning job is at hand.

Scalers are worked from the tail towards the head of the fish in short, sharp strokes, with enough downward pressure to lift and remove the scales. A knife blade doing the same job simply follows the contours of the fish.

A scaler is a handy piece of equipment because it makes a tough job fairly easy at the end of a long and bountiful day's fishing.

Top to bottom: A typical scaler and two knives with scalers on top of the blades

HAND TOOLS FOR FISHERMEN

A range of hand tools such as pliers, sidecutters, crimping tools and fish grippers are used by anglers to perform many general chores in a day's fishing.

The choice of what to carry depends on the type of angling being undertaken. All hand tools should be made of corrosion-resistant material to help withstand the attacks of salt water. All tools should be treated with a spray of WD40 or a similar compound before they even get near the water. This treatment should be repeated regularly during the life of the tools.

PLIERS

Pliers are very useful in all sorts of angling. They can be used to trim knots, cut wire, adjust lures, remove hooks, link hooks and do all sorts of maintenance jobs as needed. Every angler probably needs a good set of pliers in the tackle box.

Pliers can also be used to perform some jobs that they are not really designed for. With care, pliers can be used to close crimps and they work well as hook removers on big fish. They can also be used to close lead shot and crimp sinkers onto the line.

Pliers are also a necessary tool on every boat as part of the engine's tool kit. Given that they have so many uses, it certainly pays to spend a few extra dollars in order to have a top quality pair.

SIDECUTTERS

Sidecutters are used to cut wire and open the eyes of hooks prior to ganging. Many gamefishing anglers use sidecutters when working wire or when releasing hooked fish or sharks.

As most anglers cut wire with pliers, the sidecutters can usually be left at home, or their purchase avoided, if ganged hooks are not part of the fishing system.

Pliers and care are needed when handling the toothy barracuda.

CRIMPING TOOLS

Crimping tools come in a range of shapes and sizes for performing the basic job of closing sleeves on wire and nylon traces.

There are a large number of crimping tools on the market, of varying quality. You should avoid the super cheap and buy well-known brands.

One group of crimps that need their own hand tools are the Hi Seas and Jinkai range of nylon trace materials. These specialist items need the precision of their matching crimping pliers.

As game and sportfishing anglers can invest many hours of sweat on a fish, it pays to make traces carefully. Nothing is worse than the crimp slipping just as the trace comes to hand. Given the range of sleeves and wires available, and the precision of modern crimping tools, there is no excuse for a trace coming apart. A little care to

Crimping with pliers

make sure the right section of the crimping jaws for the size of the sleeve is used is all that is needed. The sleeve should also match the wire size.

FILES AND GRIPPERS

The other hand tool needed on every offshore boat is a file. Milled Bastard files offer the best pattern for getting hooks really sharp. Unfortunately, the files are prone to rust and need a spray of WD40 or similar after every fishing session. There are however a few good rust-proof files around and these look like an excellent answer to the corrosion problem.

Fish grippers are handy in any tackle box, yet not essential. Anglers who regularly handle a lot of flathead need good fish-gripping pliers. The same can be said for fishermen working in areas that may hold large numbers of noxious or heavily spined fish. If the crew regularly catch catfish, black trevally, red rock cod and other nasty beasties then fish grippers can be justified.

You should not however try to handle stingrays with fish grippers. The tail can come over the top of the fish and strike the hand with deadly accuracy.

PROTECTING TOOLS

Hand tools are a necessary part of the tackle box for most anglers. Their biggest enemy is salt water and they need protection in the form of a protective lubricant. There are a few stainless hand tools around and although costly they are probably worth the extra expense.

EYEWEAR
FOR ANGLERS

Sunglasses have been around for many years, although the process of manufacturing polarised lenses is more recent. It was with the advent of these polarised glasses that sport fishermen began to realise the benefits of fishermen's eyewear. Today, most keen anglers own a pair of polarised sunglasses.

The major benefits of polarised fishing spectacles are glare reduction, increased ability to see into water, reduced eyestrain, protection of the eyes from ultra-violet radiation and physical protection from hooks, rod tips, foliage and the like.

LOOKING AND SEEING

Good quality polarised sunglasses dramatically reduce the amount of reflected glare experienced by the wearer. This means that the angler is far better equipped and can look through the water instead of just seeing its reflective surface.

Quality polarised sunglasses are the next best thing to actually donning a face mask and going into the water. With good fishing glasses you will be able to see fish in relatively shallow, clear water — up to 10 or 20 metres in really crystalline conditions — watch your line, lure and bait, and detect bait fish schools. These are genuine advantages in most styles of angling.

Indeed, polarised sunglasses are so vital to certain styles of fishing that results would suffer dramatically without their use. Sand flat fishing, bluewater lure trolling, trout fishing and flathead spinning are all fishing styles in which the angler will benefit greatly from wearing polarised sunglasses.

Polarised sunglasses are essential for game fishing.

GLASS OR PLASTIC?

Fishermen's glasses come with either plastic or ground glass lenses. The plastic ones are lighter, more flexible and cheaper. They are also more prone to scratching and offer less in the way of protection.

Glass lenses are heavier, stronger, optically superior and much longer-wearing. They also tend to be a lot more expensive and prone to breakage if dropped.

If you choose glass, go for the best quality you can afford and look after them. On the other hand, if you opt for plastic, be prepared to buy a new pair every season.

CARING FOR YOUR SPECS

Keep your fishing sunglasses in a case or pouch whenever they are not in use, and never leave them where someone could sit or tread on them.

A safety strap or cord that passes around the back of your head or neck is excellent insurance against your sunnies dropping into the drink when peering into the water.

Avoid wiping your lenses with anything other than purpose-made lens cleaning tissues or a spectacle soft cloth. Shirt sleeves, handkerchiefs and even ordinary tissues can all scratch sunglass lenses. This might not be noticeable at first, but eventually results in a general 'fogging' of the image seen through the specs.

PRESCRIPTION WEARERS

Anglers who wear prescription spectacles need not miss out on the advantages offered by polarised sunglasses. Most leading manufacturers of polarised fishing glasses offer clip-on models for use in front of prescription glasses. The best of these flip up out of the way when not needed.

GET INTO THE HABIT

Get into the habit of packing your fishing sunnies or slipping a pair in your pocket as you leave to go fishing.

Even on dull or overcast days, polarised sunglasses offer very real benefits to the angler. Ultimately, they result in more enjoyable fishing and improved catches.

Polarised sunglasses help you see what is under the water.

CYALUME LIGHT STICKS

Cyalume light sticks are sticks of chemically produced light that have proved to be a boon to anglers in all manner of situations. The sticks come in a wide variety of sizes and the uses available are limited only by the angler's imagination.

The sticks remain inactive until a small glass vial within the flexible nylon tube is broken by bending. Once the two chemicals start to mix, the by-product of the reaction is light. The light has no heat or exposed power source and can operate in the water or anywhere else for that matter. The reaction produces light for four to six hours.

As the sticks are able to withstand any exposure to the elements, anglers have found a range of applications for them.

NIGHT FISHING

Night fishing anglers seeking tailor, salmon, snapper, hairtail and bream can use the tiny versions of these lights on their floats to monitor every movement their rigs make.

Rock and breakwall anglers can increase night captures with the use of the light sticks by attaching the lights close to their baits. Offshore anglers can also add the lights to their lines to attract night-feeding fish.

Artificial lights can also be used by anglers looking for mulloway, snapper and teraglin. On dark nights on offshore reefs, good results can be achieved by attaching a little beacon close to the live baits. Big fish searching the depths can see these lights

A range of Cyalume light sticks

from a long way away and will approach a struggling bait.

Given the fact that many fish also use illumination at night, the addition of a light stick does not appear unnatural and the big fish do not appear to be scared by the lights. The trolling of lures with Cyalumes in the skirts at sea has also resulted in some good catches of tuna, wahoo and marlin.

Night techniques are still the last untapped opportunity in Aussie game angling. The large longline vessels off our coast get some of their best catches in the dark, so the prospects are good for anglers prepared to venture out at night.

ACCESSORIES

Tackle manufactures have been quick to capitalise on the boom in the use of light sticks. There are a few bobby corks and floats available with fittings to hold the light sticks. But it takes very little to attach a light stick to a float anyway — a little tape and superglue will set it in place.

Special holders are also available for bait fishing rigs. These little cradles are designed to hold specific sizes of light sticks and are very handy for working tailor and hairtail with ganged pilchards. The light stick is set about 30 cm in front of the pilchard and helps the toothy ones to zero in on an obvious target.

Many anglers use the tiny light sticks on their rod tips so that they can easily keep watch for any movement, or to simply mark their outfits if setting a number of rods. The light sticks are handy for just getting around in the dark and are useful when cutting baits and tying knots and when avoiding hazards.

One vital use is in the emergency kit of an offshore boat owner. Because the sticks can be stored and require no outside power source, they can be of great value in a breakdown situation. The largest of the cyalume sticks throw enough light to be clearly seen from a long way off on a dark night.

Cyalume sticks are not expensive and should be on any night angler's shopping list.

Cyalume sticks are a real boon on night fishing trips.

FISHING FROM PIERS AND JETTIES

Jetties are the ideal place for kids to learn to fish, but they can also turn up some very good captures for more experienced hands. There are thousands of jetties around the Australian coastline, ranging from stubby, wharf-like affairs to kilometre-long structures surrounded by water deep enough to berth giant freighters.

JETTY SPECIES

What you are likely to catch from the pier in your area is largely dependent on the part of Australia you live in.

In the southern half of Australia, from Perth around to southern New South Wales, there is a certain uniformity in jetty and general inshore catches.

Although fishing piers aren't all that numerous around the southern coast of Western Australia, there are a few which have top class angling at times. Among these, Busselton Jetty is probably the best known and the most heavily fished. Herring, King George whiting, garfish and crabs are regular catches, while at the heavyweight end of the scale, mulloway, snapper and even tuna turn up.

South Australia is probably more liberally endowed with productive piers than any other state, due mainly to the sheltered nature of its gulf waters. Almost every South Oz port, regardless of size, has its own jetty, and most of these fish well for one species or another. Tommy ruff are by far the most regularly taken jetty fish in South Australia, with mullet and garfish also common. Squid, snook, whiting and juvenile salmon are also jetty specialities. During the turbulent winter months some jetties also yield snapper.

The scene is much the same in Victoria, with the exception of tommy ruff which are

A javelin fish, a common catch around tropical jetties

35

rarely taken. There are legendary tales of monster snapper being taken from the jetties in Corio Bay near Geelong, and the pier at Point Lonsdale is still famous for the shark fishing action it has produced over the years. Tathra wharf on the New South Wales far south coast and the nearby structure at Merimbula also produce a range of cool water species and the odd big shark and some game fish.

Although the jetties around the northern half of the country's coastline produce plenty of smallish species, many of these platforms are renowned for game fishing.

Tuna, big sharks, trevally, mackerel, cobia, mulloway and queenfish are all pulled from the jetties at Broome and Carnarvon in the west while the scene is much the same in central and southern Queensland, where jetties such as those at Tangalooma on Moreton Island and Urangan in Hervey Bay have a well-earned reputation for big fish action. However, most jetty anglers go looking for table fish.

JETTY TACKLE

For those anglers with their sights set on a good feed of table fish, jetty tackle need not be elaborate. Long casts are generally not required, so a medium length rod of 2 to 3 metres is ideal.

A mid-range threadline reel spooled with 4 to 6 kg line should balance nicely with such a rod, and will provide a high degree of versatility.

If there is any likelihood of tangling with a decent snapper or mulloway from your local jetty, either a sidecast or overhead outfit will be best suited. The rod should be a little bit more powerful, and 10 kg line or heavier will be a sensible option under these circumstances.

Many jetties are home to squid during the warmer months, so an artificial jig is a wise inclusion in any regular fisherman's tackle box. Blue swimmer crabs also frequent inshore waters at various times and a couple of witch's hat-style drop nets will catch these crabs right around the country.

FAVOURED JETTY BAITS

Baits used regularly by pier-based anglers vary markedly from one location to the next. Marine shellfish such as pipis and mussels are used to great effect in southern waters, and these appeal to such species as mullet, whiting, bream and salmon trout. In temperate and tropical areas prawns are as good a bait as any.

In South Australia and Western Australia, maggots are top bait for tommy ruff and garfish. Bloodworms, squid pieces and minced meat claim their share of jetty fish each year.

If snapper are on the hit list in your area, pilchards, garfish, squid strips or mullet fillets should produce results. Large green prawns are also well liked by snapper.

BERLEY FOR RESULTS

Because the jetty angler is forced to bring the fish to a fixed spot, berley can play a vital role in achieving success.

Many jetty regulars who seek Tommy ruff, mullet, silver trevally, bream or salmon trout use a berley spring or cage on their line, either attached to a light sinker or with no weight at all. An effective mixture of soaked bread and mashed chicken pellets can be squeezed into a spring. This concoction also works well when released from a berley float (feeder float) on surface feeders such as garfish.

Conversely, berley may be simply tossed into the water or dispersed from a mesh bag or old stocking hung in the water on a cord.

LURE FISHING FROM JETTIES

Many of the fish found around our jetties display at least some predatory tendencies, and will take a well-presented lure. Just which lure to use depends entirely on the available species in your area.

Lure eaters from southern Australian jetties include salmon, tailor, pike, snook, barracouta, mulloway and the odd kingfish. Tommy ruffs will also grab an artificial, but are more reliably taken with bait.

The possibilities are even greater for the northern jetty lure caster, and all manner of pelagic species are occasionally within reach. Spanish mackerel, various tunas, cobia, trevally and even billfish have been know to grab lures from piers particularly in the northwest of Western Australia.

Because jetty fishermen must operate from a fair height above the water, bibbed minnow lures are generally the most effective. They tend to run below the surface for longer than other types when worked from a high location and also have an action enticing to many inshore predators. The size of the lure used is dependent on the type and quality of fish being sought.

For southern situations, a 7 to 9 cm minnow will prove useful, while a larger lure is more applicable to fishing northern jetties. Minnows are also very effective when fished at night under jetty lights.

TIMES AND TIDES

Fish moving in the relatively shallow water around most jetties will normally feed best at dawn and dusk. There are exceptions of course, but generally speaking, a rising tide in the late afternoon or early morning will yield best results.

Snapper and mulloway are almost always better propositions after dark near jetties, but can be taken in daylight if it is overcast or the water is dirty. In South Australia, big snapper seem to bite best from the piers an hour either side of the low water at night. In Victoria, slack water at the tide change is a favoured time.

Bream, trevally and tailor are best fished on a rising to full tide, with flathead best on a falling tide.

Jetty lights attract both large and small fish at night. Squid and bait fish are fascinated by such illumination, and these in turn draw predators.

Jetties and piers provide access to some good fishing. By learning what fish frequent a jetty or pier, you can use tackle techniques and tactics that will add up to regular captures. It takes time, but then most jetties and piers are relatively comfortable and simple places to fish.

FRESHWATER TROLLING

A wide range of freshwater species — both native and exotic — can be captured by trolling lures, flies or natural baits behind a boat.

Trolling uses a moving vessel to pull a lure, fly or bait behind the boat at a speed that is attractive to the fish. Trolling requires skill and knowledge to be productive and satisfying.

There is no more effective way to fish at varying depths over wide expanses of lakes and reservoirs and in the long reaches of navigable rivers than trolling.

Some large lakes in New South Wales and Victoria contain mixed populations of exotic and indigenous species. In these fisheries, it is common for a troller trying for trout to catch Murray cod and golden or silver perch.

LURE SELECTION

There is a vast array of lures available for freshwater trolling and choosing the right ones can be difficult.

When trolling for particular species it pays to start with well-established lures that have a good reputation in a particular field. This reputation does not happen by accident — the marketplace quickly establishes which lures catch fish. If in doubt, talk to someone in the tackle store.

COLOUR

Colours should normally be close to natural, but you can also be daring. Along with natural colours, pinks, reds, silver and gold are effective.

Again be prepared to ask in a tackle store, particularly if you are in your chosen fishing area. The local tackle shop is in a great position to know exactly what is working and what is not.

See **Colour and the Angler**, pp. 20–21.

SIZE

Lure size is very much a matter of matching what the fish are eating with the size of the lure being used. For trout the basic lure sizes are well established and there is an army of available choices.

For yellowbelly and Murray cod, strong-actioned lures about the size of medium-sized yabbies seem to be the best.

On barramundi, lures which simulate a small mullet or herring get the best results.

TROLLING WITH FLIES

Wet flies such as the Red and Black Matuka, Green Matuka, Bucktail, Mrs Simpson, Muddler Minnow, Craig's Night-time, Green Whitebait and Taihape Tickler are commonly used for trout trolling.

Fly trolling is most effective when fish are feeding on the surface. An unweighted fly, trolled very slowly, 50 metres behind the boat, will take rising fish when all other lures fail.

Flies will also attract fish in deeper water. A fly is, after all, only a lure made from fur and feathers. Flies also work very well when combined with fish attractors.

FISH ATTRACTORS

In major trout lakes, trollers have found that fish attractors, otherwise known as 'Bolos', 'Ford Fenders', 'Christmas Trees', 'Cow Bells' or 'Gang Spinners', not only increase catches, but help keep the lure down without lead.

The fish attractors — hookless blades revolving around a length of wire — are more conspicuous to fish than a single lure, but they have the disadvantage of creating great tension on the line and depriving the angler of some of the 'feel' of fighting a hooked fish.

Many false strikes occur with fish attractors compared with a single lure, as fish sometimes attack the blades rather than the lure. However, fish attractors will generally produce more fish, especially in lakes and reservoirs.

Fish attractors may also be teamed with bait and flies. A hook baited with worms, a wood grub or mudeyes and tied behind a fish attractor can be devastating.

DEEP TROLLING

Impoundment fish often feed in deep water where they seek particular water temperatures. These fish are often located on depth sounders. To present a lure to these fish, a depth seeking device is needed. Many anglers use downriggers for this purpose.

TROLLING SPEED

The critical factor in trolling, likely to make the difference between productive and non-productive fishing, is trolling speed. Boat speed influences the action of the lure and affects its depth. Some lures will only work at a very slow trolling speed; the higher the speed the closer the terminal gear will be to the surface. Too much speed is the most common mistake in freshwater trolling.

Trolling speed, when seeking trout and inland natives, should be a slow walking pace: about one to one and a half knots. When trolling for northern species such as

Prime trout caught trolling with 'Cow Bells' at Lake Jindabyne

barramundi, the speed should be faster: about two to two and a half knots.

TERMINAL RIGS

Just as there are various lures and flies for different fish species, there are various terminal rigs for different trolling depths and environments.

For most freshwater trolling, the line is tied direct to a snap swivel which allows for the quick connection and changing of lures. Using the line-to-lure rig, the lure will run below the surface at the lure's operating depth. A short, nylon trace of about 25 kg is needed in tropical fresh water to cope with both the fish and the snags found in that environment. The straight line-to-fly rig can be fished on the surface or a sinker can be added to take the lure down.

Fish attractors make terminal rigs a little more complex. A main line — that is the line above the fish attractors — of about 4 kg or more is needed to withstand the drag of the attractors. When trolling for average-sized trout and native species such as golden perch and silver perch, a trace or leader of lighter line, say 3 kg, is tied between the attractor and lure, fly or bait hook. This gives the fish a sporting chance and also increases the odds of recovering the expensive attractor when only the lure is snagged. The theory is that the lighter trace, positioned between the lure and the attractor, will break before the main line rigged above the attractor.

Fish attractors impair the action of most plug-type lures when the latter are tied too near the attractors, so a leader of at least 1 metre is needed. Flies and bait hooks should be tied about half a metre away from the attractors.

Swivels are vital in any trolling rig. A keel is also important with fish attractors. On straight line-to-lure rigs, a small, snap swivel of appropriate strength should be tied between lure and line. Small plastic or lead keels are also used to minimise line twist when trolling bladed spinners.

Light to medium spinning or baitcasting gear, properly used, will handle virtually all of Australia's indigenous and exotic freshwater sportfish. In experienced hands, light gear is capable of landing even the once in a lifetime monster.

Trolling near stands of timber is nearly always successful.

FLATHEAD SPINNING

Spinning for flathead is simple yet rewarding. Well-cast lures placed in likely locations are often hit by a savage strike, ending in the capture of a tasty table fish.

Much of the fishing is visible, which adds to the excitement. The fish cannot be seen easily because of its habit of lying semi-submerged in the sand with only its eyes and mouth clear. However, the lures used can be watched through polarised sunglasses (*see* **Eyewear for Anglers**, pp. 31–2) and the strikes seen, as flathead stalk or smash the wriggling pieces of metal or plastic.

HUNTING THE HUNTERS

Flathead are active hunters, but they work from an ambush situation rather than swimming freely around the river or lake. The real skill in flathead fishing lies in selecting the spots most likely to be favoured by the flathead, and then using a lure that will trigger a strike.

A boat is a big help in covering a lot of territory, but there are plenty of places where it is possible to walk or wade and still achieve good captures. The best time for flathead spinning is in the warmer months, when the fish are more active and keen to strike.

RODS AND REELS

As the primary skill in spinning is casting lures, the choice of rod and reel is very important. The outfit must be light, cast well and be able to handle a range of lure sizes and types.

The best combination is a single-handed rod about 2 metres long, with a medium to fast taper and a light tip.

A sand flathead

The reel should be lightweight and match the rod comfortably. Lines from 3 to 5 kg are preferred, depending on the lure size being used rather than the fish being handled.

The reels can be either baitcasters or threadlines, depending on preference. Threadlines tend to be more versatile and can cast a wider range of weights and are probably the best selection.

IMPORTANT LURES

Flathead lures are chosen to perform in the various types of terrain. There is no one lure that suits all possible flathead haunts.

Small- to medium-sized deep divers are used to work drop-offs and deep channel edges. They are also handy for covering country that has a range of depths. Even in shallow water, the deep diver's habit of digging into the bottom and sending up puffs of sand can attract the fish.

THE SHALLOWS

For open sand flats, seagrass beds and general shallow water areas, very few lures are better than the Wonder or Juro Wobbler. Shallow running minnow lures are fine, as are a variety of jigs.

In a special class are the lead head jigs with their soft wriggling tails. Mr Twister-type jigs have accounted for a huge number of flathead. They cast a long way, work at any depth and can be used in particularly tough country because the hook always faces upwards, making the lures snag resistant. The seductive tail, which wiggles at any speed, makes them an ideal flathead target. The heavier jigs are best because they fish deeper. Heads of about 15 g are ideal for light outfits. Tails can be either single or double types and 10 and 15 cm versions both take fish.

CHOOSING COLOURS

Choice of colours depends on the angler, but natural looking combinations seem to work best. Lures that look just like a bait fish get treated like one.

The main exception to this is the use of fluorescent red/pink colours which are most attractive to flatties.

See **Colour and the Angler**, pp. 20–1.

Landing a flathead

FINDING FLATTIES

The real key to the whole exercise is being able to predict where the fish are most likely to be. As a fish that hunts from ambush, the flathead positions itself in places where bait fish gather or are carried by the currents.

The prime feeding time is on a falling tide, when bait is forced off the sandbanks, weed beds and flats into the channels.

Flathead set their traps on the deep edge of the channel, knowing that small fish, prawns and crabs will come past. Around weed beds they lie right on the sandy edges waiting for food to emerge. They also like to sit in any clear patches in weed bed systems. Any small creek emptying into a river or estuary system is a very likely spot.

UNUSUAL SPOTS

Flathead also specialise in hanging around unusual features in any system. A clump of rocks or weeds sitting in the middle of a sandy area will hold flathead, because it holds bait.

A fallen tree in a sandy creek will have thousands of tiny fish and shrimp sheltering in its branches, which means that flathead will be prowling close by. Rocky walls or other intrusions into the waterway are always worth a try.

In heavily tidal areas, a chain of banks and holes may develop and the flathead will work the deeper edges of these holes on the side closest to the direction of the current. As a general rule, flathead always feed with their head facing the current.

SPEEDY STRIKERS

The angler's lures need to be close to the strike zone which means within about 1 metre of the bottom. In clear water, flathead will come a long way to strike, but under normal conditions the lure needs to get close to the fish.

Despite the flathead's reputation as a passive feeder, nothing could be further from the truth. Certainly the fish will swallow a piece of old fish and sit on the bait, but when presented with live, moving prey, it can strike with blinding speed.

Any anglers hunting flathead in shallow to medium-depth water should be aware that flathead are alert and nervous and can be easily frightened. The approach to a likely spot should be just as careful as it is for trout, bass, or any other actively feeding fish.

The boat and outboard should also be used carefully, so as not to scare fish. Cast the lures ahead of the drifting boat, or out the front or back to keep the lures in areas free of disturbance from the vessel's shadow. In really likely locations, it may be wise to drop anchor and then work the lures rather than risk scaring the fish.

WHERE TO FISH

Anglers walking and wading should work the water in front of them before moving. On steeply sloping banks, the fish often lie very close to the water's edge. The angler should stand 3 or 4 metres back from the edge for the first few casts before moving up to the edge. The same applies when wading a bank edge or drop-off. Approach carefully and fish the water from far away before going close.

Fish that follow a lure can often be goaded into a strike by a rapid flick of the rod tip, which makes the lure appear to panic. Fish that strike and miss can be cast to again; if a result does not appear, then a fast lure change can be effected to try and interest the fish again.

RIGGING THE LURE

As flathead can be large and have the habit of taking a lure all the way down, it is wise to fit about 30 cm of 10 kg nylon trace joined to the main line by a small swivel. A small snap swivel can be used to link the lure to the trace. Snap swivels are of course a real boon as they allow for easy changing of lures.

Four basic spinning techniques: 1. The rod is held low and the lure retrieved a little at a time until it touches the bottom. 2. The rod is held high and the lure pulled repeatedly towards the surface. 3. A deep-diving lure is retrieved until it reaches maximum depth. 4. A plug is allowed to drift downstream; then the rod is dipped in the water and the plug reeled in under the overhanging trees.

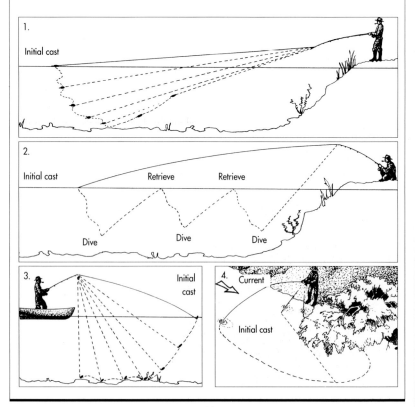

FISHING
THE WASHES

Fishing the ocean washes from a boat can open up untouched territory and increase the available fishing options. A boat has the obvious advantage of being able to cover many spots in a single session. As some of these spots will only be accessible by sea, they should therefore hold more fish.

The offshore wash areas include headlands, cliffs, bommies and islands. Wherever there are rocks and washes the following tactics for sport and game fish will work. The species may vary around the country but the techniques remain the same.

GEARED FOR THE JOB

For tackling sport and game fish near washes the basic gear usually comprises a medium-sized threadline outfit and a more solid gamefishing jigging outfit.

The threadline outfit should be about 2.2 metres in length and have a double-handed or high-winch mount to allow for easy yet powerful casting. The rod should be able to handle 6 to 10 kg line if needed. In some areas 10 kg line will be a necessity, even a bare minimum, if the average fish size is large or the terrain is tough.

The casting outfit is used for casting lures and rigged pilchards or garfish baits, and for other bait fishing applications.

The second outfit is a heavier overhead unit built along the lines of a standard jig rod and fitted with an overhead reel and 10 to 15 kg breaking strain line. This outfit is used for trolling large lures and live baiting for the big predatory speedsters that

Fighting a fish caught while spinning the washes

frequent the sudsy wash zone around offshore islands, bomboras and headlands.

The basic tackle can be supplemented with light threadlines and baitcasters or a sidecast outfit according to individual tastes.

WHERE TO LOOK

Almost all of the Australian coast has something to offer in this style of fishing. The southern areas from the Victorian border around to the end of the Great Australian Bight have less species, but there are still enough tailor, salmon, trevally, barracouta, snook and other bits and pieces to make things interesting.

Further north a great variety of species can be found and in coral country almost anything can turn up.

TACKLE REQUIREMENTS

The tackle box for this type of angling should include a range of trolling and casting lures, ganged hooks and some live baiting hooks. Add to this a few daisy chain-type bait jigs and some bait catching handlines and the gear is complete.

The trolling lures are of two types. Minnow lures are used in a range of sizes and are probably the top producers in inshore waters. A trolling pattern of several different sizes of minnows will cover almost all species found near the washes. Minnow lures can also be cast using the threadline outfit.

As an adjunct to the minnow patterns, a couple of small squids in pink and white are handy for bonito, frigate mackerel, tailor, salmon and school kingfish. Other small squid or feather lures are also useful.

Casting lures need to be of a weight that makes full-blooded, long-distance throws possible. This usually requires something of 30 to 60 g depending on the outfit. The best of the casting lures are the bait-fish-shaped lead slugs and sliced metal jigs. Heavy spoon-type lures are particularly handy on tailor and salmon and work best with a slow retrieve in and around the wash zone.

The only dead bait really needed is a block of pilchards or garfish and some berley. Live bait is added at either a known bait ground or caught on the fishing ground itself. Most washes will have some live bait available and these can be caught on either bait lines or bait jigs. Live bait is often regarded as an essential part of the system, particularly where big predatory fish such as kingies, cobia and mulloway are the target.

PRIME TIME FISHING

The prime time to fish most washes is the first few hours of daylight. This means an early start for the angler, particularly as the top bite for many fish is the piccaninny dawn, when the sun is not yet in the sky. Tailor and salmon are particularly active at these times.

The best way to find fish is to troll a pattern of lures. A combination of three minnows and one pearl-head squid fished at staggered intervals behind the boat is usually effective.

In most locations, one large minnow and two medium to small minnows make the best option. The lures are usually rigged on a 1 metre nylon trace. In the tropics, a short length of light wire may be handy.

Troll as close to the wash area as is safe using the local geography of each spot — drop-offs, bommies and so forth — to best advantage.

Watch carefully that the boat is not put in a position where it can strike a bommie or be caught by a breaking wave. If the area is not well known then approach each spot with caution.

The boat can also be used to swing the lures across a desired area by making a sharp turn once past the area to be fished. The lures will then track across the desired arc.

If fish are taken, continue trolling, or, if the bite is solid, switch to casting lures or baits. Trolling is effective but it can put the fish off fairly quickly. Often each pass will produce only a couple of fish, and then the boat is pointed towards the next headland or wash.

Watch which lures are producing, as sometimes the fish will favour a particular bait size or lure colour. If one lure is taking all the strikes, then add another just like it or change the whole combination to match the one being hit.

ALTERNATIVE APPROACH TO TROLLING

Often a spot looks fishy but trolled lures fail to produce anything. The same may apply to spots that obviously should hold fish but can't be reached with the boat.

In this situation the casting rods should be used. If distance is a problem, the boat should be used to get as close as safety will allow in order to keep the lures in the strike zone. If possible, try to mix lures with pilchards rigged on ganged hooks.

With one angler working each type of system, the fish will be located quickly if they are feeding in the area. If strikes are not forthcoming, don't stay waiting for something to happen. Move off to the next area and start again.

Most of the action will be located close to the sudsy, wave-washed areas and the baits and lures should be concentrated there. With bommies and island washes it is often possible to get right beside the surf zone without having to endanger the craft. At this distance it is easy to work the baits and lures right in the prime area.

In most fishing locations it is best to leave the motor running while working the washes. This is purely a safety precaution but it also makes manoeuvring easy.

VERSATILITY IS THE KEY

Both the lures and baits can be allowed to sink before starting the retrieve. Even though this risks snagging, many fish will lie near the bottom, particularly where the rocks meet the sand.

Both the spincasting and the bait fishing systems take mainly school fish, although the larger candidates may also get involved. To find the bigger fish on a regular basis, however, requires a more specialised approach.

LIVE BAITING THE WASHES

Live bait is the key to most of the larger fish taken around the washes. Many big fish either live or travel quite close to the coast. The deeper headlands in any area are always worth checking and offshore bommies and islands are generally reliable, big fish spots. Look for places where the current strikes the headland and deflects or moves away. These locations will hold bait and are where the big fish come looking for a feed.

The big fish system usually works best

A solid kingfish taken from the wash.

from an anchored boat, because this keeps the baits in the most likely strike zone. Live baits are set both near or on the bottom under the boat, and on the surface under a float or balloon, paid back 20 to 30 metres.

The rig for bottom live bait is a 6/0 to 8/0 Suicide hook with 1 metre of 30 kg trace running to a 100 g barrel sinker. This is loaded with a live yellowtail and lowered to the bottom. When the sinker hits bottom, it is raised about 2 metres and the rod placed in the holder with the drag set at fighting level.

The surface live bait is rigged according to the local species expected. In areas with plenty of Spanish mackerel and other critters with teeth, a short length of light wire is a good idea. In more temperate waters a couple of metres of 30 kg nylon is plenty to handle most of the inshore species.

Inshore fish are mostly under 20 kg, so the heavyweight traces used further offshore are not required. The only dirty fighters are yellowtail kings and cobia. It pays to fish the live baits on a firm drag to try and get a purchase on the fish as early as possible.

Once the live baits are set, it is normal to use some berley to help attract fish to the baits. At this time it is also worth fishing a few strip baits for table fish. Anglers can also work lures and pilchards to cover the water around the boat.

Usually most of the inshore action has shut down by about 10 am, and anglers can either turn their attention to fishing further offshore or return to the ramp to clean the catch.

BLUEWATER SPINCASTING

Spincasting is one of the most exciting forms of bluewater or offshore fishing. It is an active, hunting style of angling that provides stirring strikes and some very good catches.

The system of bluewater spincasting revolves around casting and retrieving lures from a boat, either at visible schools of fish or at locations likely to hold fish.

Places like washes, bommies, drop-offs and the like are all good spots to prospect for surface fish. Once the fish are located, lures slice through the air and a quick retrieve is often rewarded with a slashing surface strike, followed by a high speed fight on sporting tackle. The end result is either a feed or some quality bait.

TACKLE CHOICES

The major requirement of tackle in this form of angling is good casting ability. The tackle must be light yet strong, easy to work with and able to cope with the large fish sometimes encountered. Most of all it must be able to cast a wide range of lures.

Rods can be from 2 to 2.5 metres long, with a fast taper and plenty of 'backbone' for fighting stubborn fish. The rods need to have long butt sections both for ease of casting and for extra leverage when fighting fish. The butt length to the reel seat should measure about 35 cm.

There is a wide variety of suitable rods available from tackle stores. Just make sure

A high-speed baitcaster and a kingfish, a typical bluewater lure capture

the rod has high quality guides and fittings, as this type of fishing demands robust tackle.

Reels can be either overhead or threadline types, depending on personal choice. When selecting a reel for bluewater spincasting, the gear ratio must be considered carefully. Fast retrieve speeds are necessary for successful lure presentation. The faster the lure moves, the more attractive it may be to many fish. Retrieve ratios should be at least 4 to 1, and preferably 5 or 6 to 1.

PICKING LINE

Line classes can be anywhere from 4 to 10 kg depending on personal choice, the average size of the fish being sought and the type of terrain being fished. The bigger the fish and the tougher the terrain, the heavier the line that should be used.

THE LURES

Bluewater lure casting covers a lot of different territory and many fish species, so no one lure will cover all fishing situations. However, there are some basic rules that should be followed when selecting lures.

OPEN WATER

In the clear, open sea, most fish are interested in small, fast prey. The main target species are tuna which are best taken on straight-running lures retrieved very quickly.

Cut metal bar lures and sliced lures are designed to cast long distances and come through the water with maximum speed and minimum resistance.

INSHORE AREAS

Mixed schools of fish may contain tuna, bonito, kingfish, trevally, tailor, salmon, barracouta, rainbow runner, mackerel and a variety of other species, depending on location. In this situation the high-speed approach still works but it can be supplemented by using slow-moving lures which have a little action built into their design.

Leadfish and slugs are very effective. Just remember to adjust the retrieve speed to match the design of the lure. Too much pace will usually make the lure spin wildly or leap from the water.

Small- to medium-sized metal jigs (including lead lures) also work well in these areas.

WASH AREAS

Washes, bommies, coral ledges and drop-offs all provide holding areas for fish.

In southern waters these areas hold mostly salmon, tailor, kingfish and bonito, while in the tropics it is fish like trevally, coral trout, red bass, mackerel and a host of other lure crunchers that will be most often encountered. The lures used here need action and presentation rather than distance and speed.

Strong-actioned spoons in the 30 or 45 g size are excellent, as are the minnow-type lures in the 15 cm sizes. Leadfish or slug lures are also good if casting range is required.

On certain species — notably kingfish in the south and coral trout and trevally in the north — cup-faced, cigar-shaped poppers are very good for getting fish in shallow water excited.

FISHING TACTICS

Having assembled a good range of lures and suitable tackle, the angler must put together a game plan to catch fish on a given day.

To rig the tackle, a short shock leader or trace is usually necessary. This stops wear and tear from the mouth, head and gills of fish. In the areas where the fish have big, sharp teeth, a light wire trace may be necessary. A shock leader is usually about half a metre of 20 to 25 kg nylon line joined to the main line by a swivel or suitable knot.

As most surface-feeding fish school best in the early hours of daylight, anglers should start their offshore spincasting day at dawn or even earlier.

CASTING SKILLS

Wash and bommie fishing requires good casting skills. The major strike zone is close to the white water and, unless the lures are moving through the area, the angler cannot expect strikes.

The same thing applies when working coral areas. The lures must be fished where the fish live to be effective. Sometimes it means losing the odd lure to snags, but it also means catching a lot of fish.

WIDER ACTION

Moving away from the coast, the most obvious sign of surface fish activity is the presence of birds working over the school.

Terns or shearwaters are the best indicators, followed by gannets.

Birds are not the only indicator though, as fish will often be found working without any feathered company. Sharp vision and careful observation provide many strikes. Worthwhile areas include tide lines and any shallow reefs or pinnacles nearby.

Once a school of fish is located, move up to within casting distance and start work. Aim to cast the lure past the school and bring it back though the pack. Start with fast retrieve patterns and then change if necessary.

Once the school moves out of casting range, reposition the boat. Some schools are boat shy and will not come near the boat, making life difficult for anglers. In these circumstances, try to work with the sun facing you, as this will throw the boat's shadow away from the fish. Also, any breeze can be used to drift the boat towards the fish with the motor turned off.

If the fish sound, allow the cast lures to sink for 10 or 20 seconds and then start the retrieve, as the school will not be far away. Keep a good watch, and, when the fish return to the surface, the game will start again.

PROSPECT BY TROLLING

When working further offshore, the fish may be harder to locate and it is wise to troll while searching for (for example) feeding packs of tuna. Any floating object is always worth a cast for a dolphinfish or a 'rat' king.

COARSE FISHING

The term coarse fishing is not one commonly used in Australia. A coarse fisherman is one who pursues the sport of bait fishing for coarse fish, which may be categorised as all freshwater fish except trout and salmon, which are considered game fish. This form of fishing has an very strong following throughout Europe.

Coarse fishing uses bait worked under a float or with a sinker. Sinkers are known as ledgers in coarse fishing.

TACKLE

Rods for float fishing are generally between 3.5 metres and 4.5 metres in length and have an ultra-fast tip action. The extra length facilitates the use of long drops between the float and the hook.

Ledgering, or bottom fishing, without a float, requires fast taper rods ranging from 2.5 metres to 3.5 metres in length. However, if conditions allow, flick rods down to 1.5 metres long may be used where long traces (hook lengths) are not required.

Threadlines are the main reels used, although Nottingham-type (centrepin) reels are still popular for some forms of float fishing.

Most coarse fishing is done with 1 to 3 kg lines but heavier line may be used when fishing snaggy waters, or when fishing for large carp.

The long, pliant rods that are generally used for both float fishing and ledgering provide sufficient shock absorbency to land quite large fish on very light lines, although some skill is required.

Hooks most commonly used range from tiny No. 20s through to the larger end of the scale, depending on the size and type of bait being used and the species of fish sought.

Split shot is used for the precise weighting (shotting) of floats, and a range of sizes should be carried.

BAIT

The most common baits for coarse fishing are maggots, bread, sweet corn, soaked wheat and worms. Most anglers in Australia breed their own maggots though they are available at tackle shops in Victoria and South Australia.

It is interesting to note that most freshwater fish in southeastern Australia will freely take maggot baits, suggesting that maggots can be as universal a bait as worms, yet anglers rarely use them. Maggots are also deadly baits for garfish, mullet and bream.

GROUNDBAITING

Groundbaiting (or berleying) techniques are very important for coarse fishing. The berley may take the form of either cloud or particle groundbait. The former is mixed and mashed so finely that on entry to the water it forms an enticing cloud.

The choice of granular size groundbait depends on the rate of water flow and the water depth. The faster the current and the deeper the water, the coarser the groundbait needs to be to reach the vicinity of the bottom. Berley such as chicken pellets and bread and pollard frozen with wet sand are popular.

FLOAT FISHING

Float fishing involves using floats in two ways: as stick floats and as wagglers. Generally, stick floats are attached to the line at both ends of the float, whereas wagglers are attached at the bottom end only.

The basic stick float is what we would recognise as a pencil or quill float; however, varying conditions have led to the development of a multitude of designs based on this form. This range of floats is mainly used in smooth, slow to medium moving rivers of a depth of no more than 2 metres.

Shot is normally placed shirt-button style, that is, evenly spaced down the line from beneath the float down towards the bait. The float should be weighted so that only the tip is showing above the surface and any interest from the fish will be immediately signalled by the float.

Waggler floats, in contrast, are used almost exclusively in still water, lakes and very slow-moving rivers. Both stick and stem floats are used.

Shotting patterns are critical in this form of float fishing. Shotting determines the bait movement and its position in the water relative to the float. Still water fishing requires shotting that both keeps the bait at the right depth and does not alert the fish to any attached encumbrances.

Lakes often necessitate long-distance casting, in which case another requirement is that the shot be placed in such a way that the trace does not foul up the float while in flight — the bait should hit the water ahead of the float, not on top of it.

Generally, floats are shotted in such a

A coarse fisherman about to net his catch

53

way as to leave only a few millimetres of the tip showing above the surface. This amount increases the further the float is from the angler. Wagglers range from the very tiniest antennas for close-in fishing, to 40 to 45 cm missiles with weighted bodies for casting 60 metres and more.

LEDGERING

Quite simply described, ledgering is bottom fishing with a running sinker. Normally a link ledger is used, which is a running rig where the sinker is on a trace, similar to that used in some snapper fishing situations over mud bottoms. Ledger stops are either brass rings or the more common plastic tube wedges.

Another method of ledgering is to eliminate or reduce the weight and add a swimfeeder. Swimfeeders are usually celluloid cylinders with holes drilled in them, and they are filled with whatever groundbait (berley) is being used. Swimfeeders are also known as feeder floats.

There are open-end feeders, which are open at both ends for rapid groundbaiting in slower water, and block-end feeders which progressively feed in stronger currents. Although similar techniques are used in Australia, it is only in recent years that the true value of this type of berleying has been recognised.

An important part of ledgering involves the use of bite detectors. These can be in the form of well known buzzer–light types or other mechanical devices. By far the most commonly used is the quiver or nibble tip, which is a very fine length of

solid fibreglass about 15 to 45 cm long. This is attached to the tip runner of the fishing rod and creates an ultra-sensitive tip for bite detection.

These tips are available in deflection weights ranging from 14 to about 42 g and generally require a special threaded tip guide so they may be interchanged as the conditions demand. In Australia, on the estuary fishing scene, many have become aware of the incredible sensitivity of this system and some manufacturers are now marketing quiver tips.

POLE FISHING

Pole fishing has long been practised in Europe, and, however basic it may seem, there are still applications of the method which work well.

The pole has been used here in Australia for many years and is a favourite for use off jetties and rock walls. A long whippy rod with only one guide at the top — to which a length of line is attached — is used. This is commonly known as a 'Ned Kelly rig' and is a very effective way to take fish such as bream, mullet and garfish when the action is thick and fast.

The baited hook is dropped accurately into position and when a bite is felt the rod tip is lifted to set the hook. The fish is then played out by the rod tip action and lifted ashore. The single greatest advantage is being able to place the bait anywhere in the river within reach and keep it there.

The high-tech graphite poles currently available make great Ned Kelly rigs, and they do work.

CANOE FISHING

Canoes are an important still water fishing tool. They have their limitations, but they do help catch fish.

The points in favour of canoes as fishing platforms include easy mobility, a quiet approach to nervous fish, all terrain access and the combination of healthy exercise and fishing. The only major drawback is that they are not generally suitable to open water fishing.

CANOE CONSTRUCTION

Fishing canoes are generally of Canadian style, either the traditional double ender or with a cut down stern to handle a small outboard. Canoes in the 4 to 6 metre length range are ideal, though a beam of around 1 metre is necessary for stability.

Most canoes are made of fibreglass, which is robust and long lasting. Impact resistant plastic canoes are also very good.

Power is usually supplied by paddles, with either single or double blades available. The double blades are best for long stints but have the annoying habit of running water down the shaft onto the paddler. Single blades put more stress on the back and upper arms, but produce a little more power.

Outboards of various kinds are increasingly popular with canoe fishing anglers. Lightweight, electric outboards are an excellent proposition, running from four to six hours on a normal car battery. Small, petrol-powered outboards are also handy.

MODIFICATIONS

Canoes often invoke thoughts of a primitive, rugged lifestyle, but the craft need not be spartan.

Your craft can be outfitted to make fishing easier and more enjoyable. The first addition should be rubber cushions for the seats to prevent a numb or sore backside.

Large canoes make comfortable, stable fishing platforms.

Canoe shops also sell inflatable back rests to support those with bad backs.

If trolling is contemplated, small, bolt-on rod holders are available from most tackle stores. Rod holders can also be made up from lengths of 40 mm-diameter PVC pipe.

A sealable, plastic storage box is handy for jumpers, rain jackets, torches and other personal items. An ice box of some kind should also be carried.

With the rapid advance of sophisticated electronics, many really keen canoe anglers have also fitted small echo sounders or fish finders to help with fish location.

Life jackets should be carried and are compulsory in some states.

CANOE HANDLING

A large, Canadian-style canoe is relatively stable; however, some novices have balance problems and it takes a little practice and experience to get the right feel for the craft. After a while, the occupants of the canoe learn to synchronise their movements to balance each other: if one angler moves to the right the other moves to the left.

HANDLING ROUGH WEATHER

A canoe is not a perfect craft in all conditions, especially in rough water. Canoes can shoot rapids of quite startling proportions and small rapids can be quickly and safely mastered. However, care needs to be taken.

The safe way is to get out of the canoe

and carry it down to the next pool, or walk it down while holding it in the water. Only start shooting rapids once you know the terrain of the river.

It is possible to get caught in very rough conditions during storms on big lakes or in an exposed area. As with rough rapids, canoes are very good running with the wind and waves but very poor at running against them. In extreme conditions, go with the wind to the nearest point of land and then walk or get a lift back to your vehicle.

FISHING TECHNIQUES

Canoes are particularly useful to anglers who like to stalk fish. The silent running of the canoe allows many fish that might be scared or warned by the approach of an outboard to be successfully ambushed.

Most anglers using this style of fishing use lures to catch their fish; however, bait anglers can do equally well.

The canoe can also be used to simply provide access to parts of a river, lake or estuary. In addition, it can be drifted or used as a casting and trolling platform.

CANOEING FOR TROUT

Canoes are absolutely deadly on lake-dwelling trout, particularly when used to troll lures around the shoreline and near timber. Without the worry of an outboard making noises or striking a submerged object, the lures can be dragged through all the likely areas that other boats can't reach. In snaggy spots, trolling big, wet flies such as Matukas can be very useful, but standard trout lures will produce the best results.

Stalking trout using a fly rod and canoe can be very exciting. The rising fish are spotted from the boat, the canoe glides into the feeding area, and the angler gets ready to drop the fly on the next rise.

BASS ACTION

Bass anglers often use canoes to gain access to country that can't be reached any other way. Bass are caught by both lure casting and trolling, with most fish coming from snags, fallen timber and from under willow trees and other overhanging vegetation.

OUTBACK NATIVES

The streams and dams of the Murray–Darling system are excellent canoe country.

Native fish found in these waters will respond very well to cast and trolled lures, as well as baits. Like bass, most native fish are found around structures such as snags, trees and rocky drop-offs.

Often, water colouration will stop lure fishing in the outback but the canoe can be manoeuvred near the snags and a bunch of worms or a yabby can be lowered down to the unsuspecting fish below.

TROPICAL RIVERS

The magnificent rivers of northern Australia are ideal for canoe-borne exploration, except where saltwater crocs are likely to be encountered. The rivers often flow fast but are rich in fish. Sooty grunter, jungle perch, mangrove jack, barramundi, archer fish and many others inhabit these green-walled rivers. Canoeing these rivers can be a memorable experience, as the sheer beauty of the tropical rainforest streams makes them worthwhile. The fish are simply a bonus.

Most of the fish are caught on small, strong-actioned minnow or plug-type lures.

ESTUARY FISHING

Many estuary fish can be very successfully chased using canoes. A lot of shallow creeks, the ends of bays, lakes, weedy flats and mangrove creeks all yield good fishing opportunities when fished from a canoe. Both lure and bait fishing can be carried out in these spots.

Flathead and bream spinning is great sport from canoes. Using polaroid sunglasses, the lure can be clearly seen as it works its way back to the boat, only to disappear in a flurry of sand or a splash of silver. This 'hunting' form of fishing is enormously satisfying.

Mangrove creeks right around the country yield a great variety of fish to canoe anglers. Again, both lures and baits can be used and many anglers simply work with the tide, drifting upstream with a rising tide and drifting back as the tide falls.

NIGHT FISHING

Many keen daylight anglers simply don't realise how much fishing goes on at night, nor how many wonderful catches are made during the hours of darkness. It's a fact that most fish are more active around dawn and dusk, and many species extend this activity well into the night. Some fish may actually be regarded as nocturnal, doing the bulk of their hunting and feeding under the cover of darkness.

THE ESTUARY BY NIGHT

Estuary fishing after sunset is productive, and may be undertaken either from the bank or from a moored boat.

Two major targets of the night-time estuary angler are bream and mulloway.

Remember that relatively shy fish such as bream will move into surprisingly shallow areas at night in search of food. This is the time to try for them over yabby or worm-rich flats and in shallow alleys between commercial oyster leases, particularly on a rising tide. Bream will succumb to slightly heavier than normal tackle at night and this can be a real bonus around the oyster racks.

Mulloway or jewfish are a favourite of the after-dark estuary angler. The fish range from the more commonly caught soapies and schoolies of 500 g to 6 kg in weight and on up to trophies in the 15 to 40 kg bracket.

Smaller mulloway succumb mostly to cut baits, pilchards, garfish, worms, yabbies and the like, while their larger brethren prefer a strong-kicking, live bait. Remember to match your tackle to the size and power of these fish. Lines of 10 to 30 kg breaking strain are recommended, especially around structures such as bridges, jetties and breakwalls where mulloway are most often found.

A fascinating speciality of the night-time estuary angler is the hairtail, a long, chrome, silver predator with a mouthful of evil-looking fangs which invades some deeper, east coast estuaries between Townsville and Jervis Bay each winter. The renowned hot spot for this species is the Cowan Creek area of Sydney's Hawkesbury River, though great catches are also taken in Newcastle, Sydney Harbour, Botany Bay and Port Kembla at times.

BEACH AND ROCK BY NIGHT

Shore-based angling from our beaches and rocks after dark can be particularly rewarding, although, extreme caution must always be exercised on the ocean rocks. In fact, as a general rule, no spot should be fished at night until the angler has become thoroughly familiar with it during daylight hours.

Common night-time targets from the beach are bream, tailor, salmon, mulloway and sharks, while the night-shift rockhopper may add drummer, pike, snapper, sweep and even luderick to that list.

As in the estuary, slightly heavier tackle may be justified at night and often results in little or no reduction in the number of bites. For instance, rock fishermen using baits such as cunje, abalone gut and peeled prawns will often catch blackfish during the night on 6 or 8 kg line and No. 1 hooks, while the same fish may demand 2 kg traces and tiny No. 10 hooks with weed baits by day.

HEADING OFFSHORE

Setting off to sea at night has its own pitfalls, but the results often offset these. Some superb catches of snapper, mulloway, teraglin, pearl perch, tailor, samson fish and even yellowtail kingfish are made at night in southern waters, while tropical nights offer the highly prized red emperor, sea perches, sweetlips and so on. In recent years there has also been a move towards night-time game fishing for big tuna, sharks and the elusive broadbill swordfish.

Boating after sunset necessitates the use of legally required navigation and mooring lights to indicate your boat's location and travelling direction. Apart from being demanded by law, these lights make a great deal of sense if you wish to avoid being run down by a coastal steamer or another angler's boat.

Boat anglers must also be keenly aware of the increased dangers from hazards such as river bars, shallow reefs and unmarked structures during hours of darkness.

Become familiar and comfortable with your chosen waterway before tackling it at night, and always carry a powerful torch or searchlight for emergency use. Consider as well the possibility of having to stay at sea until dawn should you become lost, disoriented or denied access to your home port by sea conditions or fog.

Most night-time offshore excursions begin in the afternoon to allow the fishermen to find their marks and anchor up in a chosen location prior to nightfall. Anglers chasing mulloway, teraglin or kingfish might spend part of this time on the bait grounds catching yellowtail, slimy mackerel or similar bait fish.

Offshore tactics that work well during the day — especially the use of a berley trail in conjunction with lightly weighted floater baits — are just as effective at night. As a bonus, many hard-hit grounds commonly regarded as being 'fished out' by daytime hopefuls still produce reasonable hauls for night operators.

FRESH WATER

Many anglers fish our outback and alpine waterways at night for catfish, Murray cod, golden perch and trout.

Fly and lure anglers take some splendid bags of trout after sunset, particularly by combining the use of dark-hued and slightly larger than normal lures with a slow to dead slow retrieve.

Bass and estuary perch are also regularly taken at night on shallow running lures or, better still, surface poppers and other top artificials.

Night fishing from a jetty

In the tropics, night fishing in billabongs and semi-tidal rivers with live bait, conventional lures or poppers can provide memorable action on barramundi and saratoga, though extreme care must be exercised in known haunts of the saltwater crocodile — definitely no wading!

LIGHT AND THE NIGHT FISHERMAN

On anything other than the clearest, moonlit nights you will need artificial light of some type to assist in tasks such as rigging and re-rigging, baiting up and handling fish.

When considering lights for night fishing there are two important factors to bear in mind.

Firstly, turning on a bright light will quickly ruin your night vision by causing your pupils to contract. Assimilating to darkness again after looking into a bright light source can take as long as 15 minutes. For this reason it is best to choose a relatively soft or diffused light source for rigging and other work, and to avoid looking directly into the beam (*see* **Cyalume Light Sticks**, pp. 33–4).

Secondly, lights flashed on or across the water will often startle fish and stop them biting, at least for a time. Most fish respond quite well to a fixed or long term light source such as the illumination on a jetty or bridge, or even a bank-side campfire, but will take fright at the sudden, stabbing beam of a torch.

AFTER DARK COMMON SENSE

A few points emerge again and again when discussing safe, comfortable and productive night fishing:

• Familiarise yourself with the area during daylight.
• Carry adequate light sources.
• Move slowly and carefully.
• Don't go fishing alone.
• Keep back from the edge if shore fishing.
• Fit boats with all necessary lights.
• Tell someone where you're going and when you expect to be back.
• Anticipate having to stay out all night — carry necessary food, water and warm clothing.
• Use slightly heavier tackle than during the day.

THE TRAVELLING FISHERMAN

The world seems to be getting smaller all the time as transport systems and communication networks improve. Fishermen are increasingly taking advantage of this fact in their quest for new adventures.

It is quite within the realms of possibility for an angler reading this article in Sydney or Melbourne today to be casting a fly for tarpon in the Florida Keys, wading a Canadian trout stream or watching marlin lures dance on blue Hawaiian waters the day after tomorrow! And there are plenty of exotic fishing adventures available in Australia and neighbouring countries.

It pays to minimise the risk of disappointment, mishap or disaster by planning such excursions as thoroughly as possible.

PACKAGE TOUR OR INDEPENDENT TRAVEL?

These days, more and more operators are offering sportfishing tour packages. Some of these tour operators own lodges, fishing cabins or boats, while others act as agents for local lodge owners and skippers.

There are many advantages in taking an organised package. Arriving at a distant location with little knowledge of where to begin looking for the best fishing action doesn't make much sense. You could spend your entire hard-earned holiday just looking for a boat to hire or someone to drive you to the river!

This is not to say that it is impossible to organise your own productive sportfishing holiday. However, to do so you will need accurate, up-to-date information, and you will also need to make and confirm bookings for accommodation, boats, guides, hire cars or whatever well before you set out.

Conversely, taking advantage of a professional operator's package is not a guarantee of success, nor even of a well-serviced and happy holiday. Sadly, some tour operators have a poor reputation for providing what they promise. Worse still, fly-by-nighters occasionally come on the scene with ill-prepared set-ups, travel connections which don't eventuate or fishing craft and accommodation which fall far short of those shown in the brochure or advertisement.

Check out the operator before you book and opt for those with a proven track record. If possible, talk to someone who has undertaken the same trip you are planning and find out if they were happy with the package.

PACKING FOR THE TRIP

Make yourself a thorough check list of every item you need to take, and mark each one off as it is packed.

Try to limit the gear you take in order to reduce the weight and bulk of your baggage and try to pack versatile gear capable of fulfilling a number of functions. A big threadline reel with a spare spool may well make lots more sense than a pair of baitcasters. The same applies to lures and other items of terminal tackle. Take only those you are sure you will need and only those that you know work well. Remember, a big jig or metal lure weighs as much as three or four minnow lures.

At the end of this chapter you will find a list of tackle extras and spares to add to your list. Take particular note of the need for additional line. There is nothing worse than having all your 6 kg nylon chewed up on the coral on your first day in paradise and finding that the local store or trading post has nothing lighter than whipper snipper line!

EXPECT THE WORSE

When you pack, make sure that your bags can survive being thrown about like sacks of wheat and your rod tubes run over by baggage trolleys — chances are it will happen!

Place each reel in a cloth bag or old sock and pack them in the centre of your bag, surrounded by clothes. The same goes for tackle boxes and containers.

Rods must be stored in a sturdy PVC or plastic tube, either a commercial model or a do-it-yourself version. Pack each rod in a cloth bag before sliding it into the tube and fill any space left inside with corrugated cardboard, foam scraps or newspaper.

Clearly label every item of baggage with a tag and be sure to tear off old destination tags placed on your bags and rod tubes by airline staff.

Give some thought to insuring your tackle and camera gear, as most airlines have conservative upper limits on their financial liability for damage and loss.

Finally, relax and have a good trip.

A fishing trip is partly about getting away from it all.

THE TRAVELLING ANGLER'S CHECKLIST

One of the problems with travelling away from home to fish isolated areas is the need for a dependable and adequate supply of back-up tackle, boat and trailer spares and the like. Depending on the location you are heading for and the nature of the fishing you'll be doing there, other tools or tackle items may also need to be added to the basic travelling angler's checklist below.

Tackle Extras
Spare spools of line (one per reel)
Wire and heavy nylon trace material
Spare hooks, including trebles, and
    heavy duty rings
Hook remover
Wire cutters
Crimping tool
Nail clippers (for cutting line)
Ball bearing swivels and snaps
Scales (for weighing fish)
Bobby corks and/or balloons
Bait catching rigs
Heavy handline
Landing net
Hand gaff
Squid jig
Log book and pen (for recording catch
    details)

Tackle Repair Kit
Glues (two-part epoxy and superglue)
Electrical tape
Spare runners
Spare tip guide (bind-on type)

Clear nail polish
Binding thread
Spare bail springs for threadline reels
Light reel grease

Boat Repair Kit
Spark plugs
Spark plug wrench
Spare sheer pin (if applicable)
WD40 or similar spray lubricant
Spare fuel line
Multi-grip pliers
Electrician's long-nosed pliers
Spare fuses
Screwdrivers
Spare prop
Wrench
Spare boat bungs

Trailer Repair Kit
Spare tyre
Emergency tyre inflator
Foot pump
Spare tyre valve
Jack
Spare shackle
Spare bearings
Grease
Spare globes for tail lights

Safety Essentials
Hat
Sunscreen (maximum protection factor)
Polarised sunglasses
Insect repellent
First aid kit
Spare sandshoes

INDEX